LIGHT
SHINING
THROUGH THE
MIST

L·I·G·H·T
SHINING
THROUGH THE
M·I·S·T

A PHOTOBIOGRAPHY
OF DIAN FOSSEY

by Tom L. Matthews

NATIONAL GEOGRAPHIC SOCIETY

WASHINGTON, D.C.

FOR BARBARA
Time is *the best storyteller.*

Published by the
National Geographic Society
1145 17th St. N.W.
Washington, D.C. 20036

Staff for this book:

Barbara Lalicki
Project Director

Marianne Koszorus
Art Director

David M. Seager
Designer

Barbara Brownell
Senior Editor

Carl Mehler
Senior Map Editor

Suzanne Fonda
Editor

National Geographic Maps
and Jehan Aziz
Map Production

Jennifer Emmett
Assistant Editor

Elisabeth MacRae-Bobynskyj
Indexer

Vincent P. Ryan
Manufacturing Manager

Lewis R. Bassford
Production Manager

Library of Congress Cataloging-in-Publication Data
Matthews, Tom L., 1949–
    Light shining through the mist : a photobiography of Dian
Fossey / by Tom L. Matthews
        p. cm.
    Includes bibliographical references and index.
    Summary: Traces the adventurous life of the American
woman who worked as a zoologist among the mountain gorillas of the
Virunga area of central Africa.
    ISBN 0–7922–7300–1
    1. Fossey, Dian—Juvenile literature.   2. Gorilla—Rwanda—
Juvenile literature. 3. Primatologists—United States—Biography—
Juvenile literature. [1. Fossey, Dian. 2. Gorilla.
3. Zoologists. 4. Women—Biography.] I. Title.
QL31.F65M38
599.884'092—dc21 97–34084   CIP

Printed in the United States of America

I HAD A DEEP WISH TO SEE AND
LIVE WITH WILD ANIMALS IN A WORLD
THAT HADN'T YET BEEN COMPLETELY
CHANGED BY HUMANS. I GUESS I REALLY
WANTED TO GO BACKWARD IN TIME....
THE THOUGHT OF BEING WHERE THE
ANIMALS HAVEN'T ALL BEEN DRIVEN INTO
LITTLE CORNERS ATTRACTS ME SO MUCH."

▲*Dian Fossey was the first human being to get this close to a mountain gorilla without her or the gorilla being frightened.*

FOREWORD

ONCE, LONG AGO, I STUDIED MOUNTAIN GORILLAS. THE SIGHTS OF THE majestic males and exuberant youngsters still remain as treasured memories. Dian Fossey continued this research on gorillas, the most powerful and elegant of the apes. Indeed she devoted her life to them.

Dian had never done a field study before. Yet her mind was filled with curiosity and a sense of wonder, the most important attributes for anyone intrigued by nature. Soon she learned to know gorillas as individuals, looking at them almost as family. She treated them not as inferior beings but as creatures with feelings, imagination, and awareness. In this way she immersed herself in the gorillas' world. It enabled her to contribute importantly to scientific knowledge.

Gorillas are our kin, mirrors of ourselves, closer to us than any other creature except the chimpanzee. Dian's intimacy with them helped start a quiet revolution of friendly relationships with wild animals.

But Dian Fossey's contribution went far beyond that. She watched as the gorillas' forest home was cut down and the animals were wantonly killed by local people. With selfless dedication she made it her mission to protect the gorillas. She pursued her cause with such passion, persistence, and compassion that she ultimately gave her life to it. Through her heroic vigil the world became aware of the gorillas' plight. By her example she taught us all an important lesson: We must be willing to share the earth with all forms of life, and we must be willing to fight for this belief.

Gorillas have had a desolate time in recent years as civil war has engulfed their homeland. So far they have endured, but their future remains uncertain. Others are now continuing the effort to save them, an effort that must continue forevermore because they will never be wholly safe.

George B. Schaller
Wildlife Conservation Society
New York

▲ *Dian got along well with people her own age, but friends say that she cared most for animals. As a child, the only pet she ever had was a goldfish. Years later, Dian remembered how terrible she felt when the fish died. She wrote: "I cried for a week."*

$\mathbf{D}$IAN FOSSEY WAS BORN IN 1932, in San Franciso. In those days Americans were struggling with the Great Depression and didn't have money to put aside for insurance. So George Fossey, a tall, easy-going man who loved his daughter and loved being outdoors, wasn't very successful selling insurance. Failure depressed him and he drank too much. Drinking led to trouble with the police and divorce from Kitty, Dian's mother, when Dian was six.

A year later, Kitty married Richard Price, a successful building contractor. Richard Price never adopted Dian so she kept the name Fossey. Even so, she always called her stepfather "Daddy."

Dian's petite mother had been a professional fashion model. She was very concerned about Dian's looks. Dian was six feet tall by her late teens, and it disturbed Kitty that her active, attractive daughter continued to grow taller than a girl had any reason to grow.

▶ *Like many parents, Dian's mother, Kitty, and her stepfather, Richard Price, were concerned about their daughter's future.*

FINALLY I REALIZED THAT DREAMS SELDOM MATERIALIZE ON THEIR OWN."

▲ *One summer Dian landed a job on a dude ranch in Montana, where she rode horses all day long. She called it "the best job I ever had."*

After high school, her parents wanted her to study business. Dian tried it and hated it. At another college, she studied veterinary medicine, her real love. To pay for tuition and living expenses, she worked weekends, holidays, and summers.

Dian excelled in the study of plants and animals, but failures in physics and chemistry doomed her career as a veterinarian. She chose another— occupational therapy—working with physically- and mentally-challenged children. She graduated from San Jose State in 1954 and worked in a number of hospitals before landing a job in Louisville, Kentucky, at Kosair Children's Hospital. As Director of Occupational Therapy, she worked with autistic children. Their disease makes them shy, untalkative, and fearful. Dian wrote, "These children have a variety of physical and emotional disabilities and are lost in this world of ours....They need a tremendous amount of care and kindness to make them feel life is worth living."

Dian cared deeply and worked hard and lived quite happily in a run-down farm cottage where she was surrounded by animals.

She made good friends and dated men who found her extremely interesting, but she wasn't strongly attracted to any of them.

She was more attracted to a dream: traveling to Africa.

Her best friend, Mary Jo White, planned a safari to Africa in 1960 and offered to pay Dian's way. Dian desperately wanted to go, but couldn't take that big a gift, even from a friend.

▶ *Mary Jo White visited East Africa's sun-drenched Serengeti Plain (below) where antelope and lions and elephants roam free—the Africa of Hollywood movies.*

Instead, she began "saving every penny for Africa," and eventually took out a high-interest loan to pay for a trip to Kenya and Tanzania, in East Africa. She could have asked her generous Uncle Bert in California for help, but she was too independent to borrow from family. Dian hoped to pay off her debts quickly by writing travel articles illustrated with her own wildlife photographs.

◀Throughout history, the mountain gorilla has been a victim of bad publicity caused by the lack of firsthand knowledge.

Then she found a book by George Schaller about his year studying mountain gorillas. He said that gorillas weren't violent, nightmarish creatures. They were shy, gentle giants. Not naturally aggressive toward humans. Vegetarians!

Fascinated, she added a side trip to photograph gorillas living on the two-mile-high peaks of the Virunga Mountains.

Dian's African adventure began September 26, 1963. Just to be safe, she carried a 44-pound bag of emergency medical supplies.

Those supplies came in handy. By the time her plane reached Egypt, Dian was sick. She was dazed and confused by the frenzy of travel and the strange sights, sounds, and smells. Dian's relationship with her hired guide started badly, and then got worse. For a month they argued over routes to take, lateness, money, everything. But nothing could take the shine off Dian's trip. She was in awe of the wildlife, the regal Masai tribespeople, and the spectacular, unspoiled scenery.

Her guide drove on to Tanzania's Olduvai Gorge. Dian had the ridiculous hope of speaking with Dr. Louis Leakey, a world-famous anthropologist who rarely gave interviews to professional reporters when he was in the field. And Dian was no professional reporter.

▶Dr. Louis S. B. Leakey and his wife, Mary, spent decades in East Africa digging for fossils that revealed some of the four-million-year history of humankind. Because people are closely related to the great apes, he thought that the behavior of chimpanzees, orangutans, and gorillas would help us understand how early humans lived.

At first sight, she charged the 60-year-old scientist like a teenager rushing a concert stage. Unshaved and caked with dust, Leakey was unexpectedly charming. Dian mentioned the Virunga gorillas and Leakey asked, "Are you merely interested in gorillas as a spectator or as a journalist?"

"Much more than that, Dr. Leakey. Someday I plan to come here to live and work." She had never stated that goal to anyone before; never written it in her journal. Was it a surprise to her when she said it? Or a dream spoken out loud?

Rushing about to take pictures of Leakey, she slipped and wrenched her ankle very badly. After bandaging the ankle, the Leakeys sent Dian on her way but said, "Keep in touch."

Determined to see gorillas, Dian headed west with her guide into Uganda, to the famed Travellers Rest hotel at the base of the Virunga Mountains. The hotel owner, Walter Baumgartel, suggested hooking up with two wildlife photographers, Joan and Alan Root.

It took Dian nearly seven hours of tortuous climbing on a swollen ankle to reach the Roots' camp 11,400 feet above sea level on Mount Mikeno. Even without the sprain, Dian was not a natural for gorilla spotting in thin mountain air. She suffered from asthma attacks, and her lungs were scarred from smoking. Several different allergies gave her high fevers and made her face balloon.

Two days of searching passed with no sign of gorillas.

Then it happened.

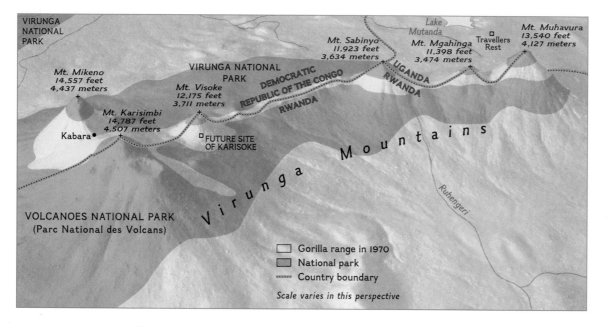

▲*Mountain gorillas avoid open plains and meadows. Their known habitat in 1970 (shown in yellow) was roughly 35 miles long and as wide as 12 miles. They range freely across the borders of the Democratic Republic of the Congo, Rwanda, and Uganda.*

▶ *The Virunga Mountains are one of earth's most exotic habitats: rainy, cold, and green all year round. Sunlight filtered through mist covers these peaks in deep purples and blues.*

"THE TERRAIN WAS UNBELIEVABLE, ALMOST STRAIGHT UP, AND WE HAD TO HANG ON TO VINES TO GET ALONG OR GO ON HANDS AND KNEES."

The African camp cook stood awestruck by his first sight of gorillas and whispered, *"Kweli nudugu yanga!"* in Swahili: "Surely, God, these are my kin."

Kin: Related by blood, family. Mountain gorillas are part of the same group of primates we humans belong to—the great apes.

It was the cook's first face-to-face look at a gorilla for two reasons.

▼ *Some of the adult males Dian saw probably weighed nearly 400 pounds. They were nearly six feet tall standing upright. But they were more comfortable walking with their knuckles on the ground, pulling at the plants to drag their weight forward.*

First, most Africans believed in the ancient tales of gorilla strength, cruelty, and savagery. Second, it was easy to avoid them.

All mountain gorillas known then, fewer than 400 individuals, lived around the Virunga volcanoes in central Africa. They ate, rested, and played in small family groups that traveled many miles each day through dense forest.

After the fear and excitement passed, Dian had a deeper reaction to her first gorilla sighting. "I left Mount Mikeno [the] next day, never doubting that somehow I would return to learn more about the Virunga gorillas."

I SHALL NEVER FORGET MY FIRST ENCOUNTER WITH GORILLAS.... SOUND PRECEDED SIGHT AND ODOR PRECEDED BOTH IN THE FORM OF AN OVERWHELMING, MUSKY, BARNYARD YET HUMANLIKE STENCH. THEN THE THIN MOUNTAIN AIR WAS SHATTERED LIKE WINDOW GLASS BY A HIGH-PITCHED SERIES OF DEAFENING SCREAMS.... WE ALL FROZE....A GROUP OF ABOUT SIX ADULT GORILLAS STARED...BACK AT US....THEIR BRIGHT GAZES DARTED NERVOUSLY FROM UNDER THEIR HEAVY BROWS AS THEY TRIED TO DETERMINE IF WE WERE DANGEROUS."

▲ *Dr. Leakey, Kenyan by birth, was also a jet-hopping lecturer. His field research was expensive, so international speaking tours helped pay the bills, along with funds from conservation groups, governments, and the National Geographic Society.*

Back home in Kentucky, Dian worked at the hospital, lived in her cabin. She produced a number of magazine articles about her trip—all rejected. She wrote a children's book about Africa but couldn't sell it. Finally, the local paper published three articles. They made her a hometown celebrity, but Dian was drifting.

Then Louis Leakey came to Louisville in March 1966 on a lecture tour. Dian sat in the filled hall, clutching copies of her articles. After the program, as she stood in line to greet him, his eyes caught hers. "Miss Fossey, isn't it?" he asked. "Please wait until I've finished with all these people."

The next afternoon they talked at length. He had the power to offer her a job observing gorilla behavior, but she told him why he shouldn't: She wasn't trained in behavioral science….Leakey had no use for over-trained people. She couldn't raise money to pay for the study….Leakey could. She was too old—34….Leakey said, "But this is the perfect age to begin such work."

He didn't offer her the position, but said he'd write. Dian spent months fretting anxiously. And then the letter arrived.

Leakey had obtained funding from the National Geographic Society and the Wilkie Brothers Foundation. He offered her a three-year position to study mountain gorillas, if she wanted it. She did.

In late December 1966, good-byes all said, she arrived again in Africa. Dian and Leakey shopped, gathering the essentials for life in the wild—food, clothes, blankets, a shortwave radio, gas for reading lamps, and a secondhand Land Rover. She would be staying at Kabara, where George Schaller had studied mountain gorillas. Alan Root, the photographer she had met in 1963, drove with her to the Congo to "make sure I at least reached the right country."

▶Leakey recruited Jane Goodall to do a long-term study of chimpanzees at Gombe Preserve, in Tanzania. This study was so successful that Leakey was looking for someone to study mountain gorillas in the Virungas.

Dian had prepared by studying scientific texts and learning the native language, Swahili, from a phrase book. But a modern American can hardly prepare to work and live alone for years without electricity, central heat, or even running water. If the campfire went out, there was no boiling water for baths or washing clothes.

▼The odds against Dian Fossey's success were high. Her weak, scarred lungs were no match for the climate. She lacked formal scientific training as a zoologist or field researcher. She had to learn on the job. And she was alone.

After two weeks, Root left camp satisfied that Dian's enterprise was up and running as well as possible. Reality closed in like the mist. "I'll never forget the feeling of sheer panic that I felt watching him depart. He was my last contact with civilization as I had known it. I found myself clinging to the tent pole simply to avoid running after him....I couldn't read any of the popular or scientific books I'd brought, or even use my typewriter. All of those connections with the outside world simply made me feel lonelier than ever."

She focused on work. Dian and Sanweke, her Congolese tracker, would take thermoses of tea into the forest and search from early morning until sunset. She heard gorillas in the forest for weeks before sighting one. Then came the trial and error, seeing what worked. It would take a long time, but she had three years worth of funding and the Congo's internal troubles would never reach her tiny mountain camp.

▼ *Incredibly shy by nature, these gorillas are keeping a safe distance between themselves and Dian.*

▲ *All three countries that contain mountain gorilla habitat—the Congo, Rwanda, and Uganda—have been devastated by civil wars that have resulted in thousands of casualties and sent millions of refugees back and forth across the borders. Miraculously, the endangered gorillas have survived human chaos and tragedy.*

By July 1967, full-scale civil war engulfed the Congo. Dian was taken from her camp by army guards and held under arrest for weeks. Finally, she talked the guards into taking her to the Travellers Rest, where she pretended to have money hidden to pay for a "security bond," or bribe. She was desperate to escape.

At the door of Walter Baumgartel's hotel, she charged inside and hid under a guest bed. An embarrassed soldier said he would be executed if he went back to the Congo without Fossey.

"Better to shoot you than her," Baumgartel replied.

Unable to return to Kabara but unwilling to give up her study, Dian decided to set up camp in Rwanda's Volcanoes National Park, a refuge for gorillas and other free-living animals.

She found a beautiful, level spot in the saddle between Mount Karisimbi and Mount Visoke. She combined the names into Karisoke, and the empty field became the Karisoke Research Center.

Karisoke started with a tent to sleep in, barrels to catch rainwater for drinking, a ditch for a communal toilet, and a routine. Rising at 5:30 a.m., Dian tracked gorillas until dusk. At night, she laundered and hung her clothing to dry, fired her gas lamps, and spent hours typing notes and reading scientific books. The sounds of elephants, buffalo, and antelopes wandering through the meadow were her nightly entertainment.

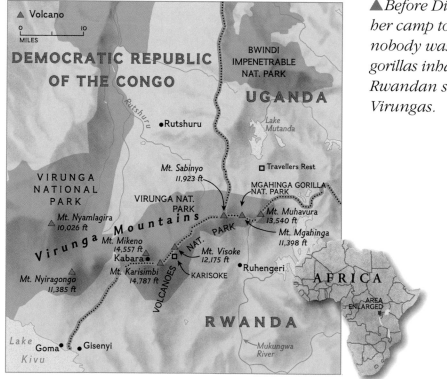

▲Before Dian moved her camp to Karisoke, nobody was certain that gorillas inhabited the Rwandan side of the Virungas.

Her new cook and trackers were Rwandese and spoke
Kinyarwanda, a language that relies on vocal inflection and body
language. It's so difficult for foreigners to learn that she and her
staff settled for a little Swahili and a lot of hand signals.

George Schaller's study had explained the range behavior of gorillas—
how they moved in groups, how much they traveled, what they ate.
He established the "rules of contact"—how to behave to get near
enough to observe the gorillas without frightening them.

Dian's goal was to get as close to these giants as her colleague Jane
Goodall had gotten to their much smaller cousins, the chimpanzees.

▼ *Whatever needed
doing—sewing,
cooking, or chopping
wood—was done by
Dian and her cook,
the camp's only full-
time workers.*

She wanted to learn about their social interaction — how they acted together when they weren't being observed. And the only way to see how gorillas acted when they weren't being watched was to be accepted as a gorilla.

She aped, or imitated, gorilla behavior. Dian would crouch in the soaking-wet vegetation for hours in plain sight of a group. She would knuckle-walk around them, but keep her eyes turned away, never staring. She groomed herself and made day nests to rest in and pretended to munch on gorilla delicacies like wild celery and bamboo. Sometimes, sensing distrust in the gorillas eyes, she really chewed and swallowed the food!

Covering miles of steep, slippery ground with her trackers each day, Dian learned to recognize groups of gorillas and individuals within each group by nose prints. She identified nine different groups, which she numbered 1 through 9. All gorilla family groups are led by silverbacks — adult male gorillas with unique growths of white fur on their backs.

◄ *"Why should I apologize for saying it's always cold here?" Dian wrote. Note the heavy gloves and coat she wears as she crouches in the vegetation while aping gorilla behavior— eyes averted, pawing at food.*

▶ *The ridges and furrows of each gorilla's face are unique, just as our fingerprints are unique. Identification starts with rough drawings that become more detailed over months of building trust and slowly getting closer and closer to an individual.*

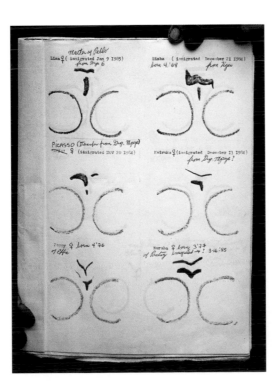

At first Dian had the most contact with Group 4, and they were her favorites. She named its silverback leader Whinny because of the horselike whinnying sounds of alarm he made. She called a younger silverback Uncle Bert, "but my uncle never quite forgave me." Old Goat and Mrs. X were the names she gave the eldest females, and Digit was a lively, adolescent male named for his permanently twisted, broken finger.

Group 8 was unique because it had no babies to protect and quickly accepted Dian's presence. The group's ancient silverback she called Rafiki — "friend" in Swahili. Geezer and Peanuts were two extremely playful young males.

◄ Old Goat, the senior female of Group 4, carries an infant on her back. All babies are carried this way until they can keep up with the group. Some are carried until they are four or five years old.

► Dian climbs a giant hagenia tree to examine a night nest. Mountain gorillas build new nests every night, usually closer to the ground than this one.

▶ *Dian reviews a day's work outside the cabin she called home for nearly 18 years. Wood is chopped for the campfire that never went out.*

Eventually, she built a cabin with two rooms. "It was always a most delightful, cozy feeling to type up field notes near the crackling fireplace at night with...the sounds of the owls, hyrax, antelope, buffalo, and elephant outside."

But Dian wasn't alone with her helpers and the wild animals.

Volcanoes National Park is a gorilla sanctuary, but Rwanda wasn't doing much to protect gorillas in 1967. Some of the park was used for farming. Herdsmen let cattle graze on gorilla land. And the native forest-people poached — illegally hunted and killed — animals in the national park.

◄Dian destroys a bamboo trap. Hundreds are set to ensnare bushbuck and duiker, small forest antelope. When gorillas are trapped by mistake, the results are horrible. They break away with broken and cut arms and legs. Their mangled limbs become infected, gangrene sets in, and the wounded gorillas die.

Some poachers actually meant to trap or kill gorillas. *Sumu*, a Swahili word used in Rwanda to mean "black magic," was a powerful motive for killing gorillas. A magic potion made from boiled gorilla gave its drinkers the strength of the gorilla, they thought.

Gorillas were also hunted for body parts. Collectors paid thousands of dollars to have a gorilla head in the family room or an ashtray made from a gorilla's hand in the office.

Capturing infant gorillas alive for zoos caused the most destructive poaching. A gorilla group will not allow its young to be harmed under any circumstances. In order to capture an infant, many other gorillas in the group had to be killed.

As a scientific observer, Dian wasn't supposed to "intervene." The times she did want to, it was physically impossible. Gorillas are incredibly protective of group members. To approach and handle a sick gorilla, she would have had to tranquilize an entire group.

But if the government of Rwanda couldn't or wouldn't protect the gorillas in a park created for their protection, Dian would. She called her crusade "active conservation."

First she warned the poachers and cattle herders. After warnings failed, she destroyed poachers' traps and drove cattle out of the park.

Native Rwandese were angry about the foreign woman's interference in their business. Even Dian's friends were upset. One said, "These men have a right to hunt. It's their country! You have no right to destroy their efforts."

Dian was not swayed. She had to protect the gorillas.

"IF I CAN ENFORCE THE WRITTEN RULES OF A SUPPOSEDLY PROTECTED PARK AGAINST THE SLAUGHTER OF ANIMALS, THEN I MUST DO IT."

◀ *Gorilla hands are displayed in a* sumu *shop. Many items sold here cost the lives of endangered species.*

▲*An infant grabs a treat while sitting on its mother's back. Mountain gorillas feast on more than 75 kinds of leaves, roots, and berries. They occasionally eat insects for protein, but no fish or meat, ever.*

In March 1969, Dian learned that an infant gorilla was being held at park headquarters. It had been captive in a dark, almost airless box for six weeks and was desperately ill. The baby gorilla had been captured for a zoo in Europe.

Ten members of the infant's group were killed trying to protect her.

To get control of the gorilla, Dian agreed to give the baby to park officials as soon as it was healthy enough to travel. She called her patient Coco.

Coco's arrival in camp was like a tornado passing through a sleepy, small town. Dian turned her cabin into a jungle to make Coco comfortable. Trackers were detailed to find fresh gorilla food for Coco. The camp cook quit in protest, insulted by the idea of making "gorilla meals."

Instead of a miracle happening to make things better, another infant gorilla, this one in worse shape than the first, was dropped on her doorstep. Pucker was emaciated, oozing pus from panga, or machete, wounds on her head. She was raw all over from being tightly bound by cutting wire. Pucker, too, was destined for zoo life if she survived.

With two animals in need of constant attention, Dian became a full-time nurse, and her fieldwork stopped. But her understanding of gorilla behavior soared as she slowly brought the infants back to health.

▶ *This nest, a shelf covered with vegetation, is one of the areas Dian created in her cabin to help keep the house-bound infants occupied.*

32

She was able to observe their feeding habits, grooming, and vocalizations at close range. She learned what their sounds meant to each other and, presumably, to other gorillas.

All the while, Dian pleaded her case to keep the babies — they could be returned to the wild and placed, like orphans, with new gorilla groups.

Coco and Pucker eventually were packed up and flown to a zoo where they lived for several years and died before reaching maturity. No mountain gorilla has ever had babies or lived a full life in captivity.

I RAN OUT OF THE CABIN...

DEEP INTO THE FOREST UNTIL I COULD RUN

NO MORE. THERE IS NO WAY TO DESCRIBE

THE PAIN OF THEIR LOSS."

◀ *The intimacy Dian developed with Coco and Pucker opened a window on new scientific horizons. She discovered how gorillas communicate with each other and what they are saying to each other.*

▶ *Dian grooms Coco as Coco grooms Pucker. Grooming is an important social activity that gorillas learn from their mothers (or substitute mothers) during infancy.*

Rushing back into fieldwork, Dian was eager to see if the phrases she learned from Coco and Pucker meant the same things to all gorillas. Encountering Group 8 first, she saw Rafiki and croaked out *Naoom, naoom, naoom*, a phrase equivalent to "Food is served, come and get it."

Rafiki's reaction was stunning. He moved toward Dian, staring intently as if to say, "Come on now, you can't fool me!"

There was more meaning to a *naoom* than food, she soon learned. This "belch vocalization" is a way for gorillas to tell others they are happy and content. Group members belch back. It helps them keep track of where everybody is while sitting in dense vegetation. Dian used this sound to approach groups without startling them, and they readily accepted her "gorilla-ness."

▲ *Dian recorded dozens of hours of gorilla vocalizations as part of her fieldwork.*

The hoot bark is a sound of curiosity or general alarm. When a silverback hoot barks, he gets everyone's attention. For example, a silverback will *wraagh* when entering another group's territory to say: "It's only us. Don't worry."

A short belch is used to discipline the young. A pig grunt is used by silverbacks to settle disputes among other gorillas. Females use it to discipline their young or settle arguments over food, and the young use it among themselves to complain about rough play.

Dian discovered that gorillas use at least 25 different vocalizations to communicate.

People who find work that they love are very fortunate. Gorillas were both Dian's job and her love, but external demands stole her away from fieldwork for academic work. She needed a Ph.D.— her "union card"—to be a recognized expert.

In the fall of 1969, she visited Cambridge University to meet with her advisor and plan a course of study. She thought Cambridge was dark, noisy, crowded, and too fast-paced, but she would have to spend several months there each year taking courses before returning to her fieldwork in Rwanda.

Before starting her first semester, Dian was able to fly back to Karisoke for her favorite holiday, Christmas. After the celebrations were over, she went out to track Group 8 one last time. Almost immediately she found Peanuts, the most playful gorilla she knew.

Dian recorded this stunning moment in her journal. "Peanuts left his tree for a bit of strutting before he began his approach. He is a showman. He beat his chest; he threw leaves into the air; he swaggered and slapped the foliage around him; and then suddenly he was at my side. His expression indicated that he had entertained me — now it was my turn.

I SCRATCHED MY SCALP NOISILY....

ALMOST IMMEDIATELY PEANUTS BEGAN TO SCRATCH.

IT WAS NOT CLEAR WHO WAS APING WHOM."

P EANUTS SEEMED
TO PONDER
ACCEPTING MY
HAND....[AND] GENTLY
TOUCHED HIS FINGERS
TO MINE....
TO THE BEST OF MY
KNOWLEDGE, THIS IS THE
FIRST TIME A WILD
GORILLA HAS EVER COME
SO CLOSE TO
'HOLDING HANDS' WITH A
HUMAN BEING."

After this moment with Peanuts,
Dian wrote, "This was the most
wonderful going-away present I could
have had."
Filled with joy and triumph, she left
for Cambridge.

41

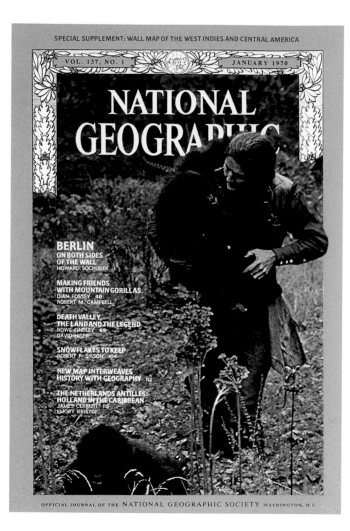

SPECIAL SUPPLEMENT: WALL MAP OF THE WEST INDIES AND CENTRAL AMERICA

VOL. 137, NO. 1   JANUARY 1970

NATIONAL GEOGRAPHIC

BERLIN
ON BOTH SIDES
OF THE WALL
HOWARD SOCHUREK   1

MAKING FRIENDS
WITH MOUNTAIN GORILLAS
DIAN FOSSEY   48
ROBERT M. CAMPBELL

DEATH VALLEY,
THE LAND AND THE LEGEND
ROWE FINDLEY   69
DAVID HISER

SNOWFLAKES TO KEEP
ROBERT F. SISSON   104

NEW MAP INTERWEAVES
HISTORY WITH GEOGRAPHY   112

THE NETHERLANDS ANTILLES:
HOLLAND IN THE CARIBBEAN
JAMES CERRUTI   115
EMORY KRISTOF

OFFICIAL JOURNAL OF THE NATIONAL GEOGRAPHIC SOCIETY WASHINGTON, D.C.

◄ *The article featuring Coco and Pucker inspired hundreds of would-be volunteers to write to Dian and offer their services at Karisoke.*

Dian had a second present that January—the cover of NATIONAL GEOGRAPHIC magazine. She and the gorillas were instant international celebrities.

To raise money for Karisoke, Dian had to travel more—making speeches, giving progress reports, and talking at fund-raising events. Her very first public-speaking event was a $1,000-a-plate dinner for the Leakey Foundation. People said her talk was unforgettable.

Fame had its downside. Film teams and curious tourists arrived at Karisoke unannounced and uninvited. Strangers pitched tents and demanded tours. Some tourists bribed park officials to get private showings of gorillas.

Students wanted to come and assist, but many found it difficult to live at high altitude in the Virungas—closed in by the cloud-like mists, drenched by soaking rain, cut off from friends and family. Dian called it the Astronaut Blues. Yet, over time, dozens of graduate students assisted Dian in census taking, sound recording, and statistical work.

Whenever Dian traveled to Europe and the U.S., she couldn't resist two indulgences. She shopped for fashionable new outfits and spent as much as she could afford on presents to be hidden until the annual Christmas celebrations at Karisoke.

▶A gorilla census crew dries their "gear" after days of rain. The man third from the left is a Rwandese university student, one of several Africans who did fieldwork at Karisoke.

Karisoke was decorated for Christmas with garlands made from tinfoil and popcorn, and other homemade ornaments. Students came, but, to Dian, African staff members and their wives and children were the important guests.

They came to feast, to dance, and to sing carols in Kinyarwanda, French, and English. The African parents shared Dian's delight in watching their children figure out gizmos, gadgets, and toys made for Western children. Those parties were magical for Dian.

▶Ian Redmond studied gorilla parasites and led the anti-poaching patrols at Karisoke. Far right: He and Kelly Stewart, another student, celebrate a Karisoke Christmas.

During the 1970s, Dian's cabin became the foundation for a small village of cabins, year-round tents, outhouses, a smokehouse, a chicken house, and even a laundry.

But even though the center grew in size and international stature, money always had to be raised to keep it going. In the entire 18 years she worked there, Dian never earned a salary. Quite often, she paid trackers and bought food with her own savings. When her Uncle Bert died and left Dian $50,000, her first thoughts were that the money could keep Karisoke running for three years.

◀ It is easy for gorillas to travel the montane forest, but slow going for people. Dian's regular conferences with trackers updated group movements so gorillas could be found without days of frustrating searching.

◀ Dian examines and catalogs gorilla bones found in the forest. Bone studies helped determine how gorillas died. Was it disease, violence, or old age? The principal killers of adult gorillas, she found, are respiratory diseases like pneumonia.

Every aspect of work and play at Karisoke was important and received Dian's meticulous attention.

Once she used old car tires to make a pair of boots by hand for a tracker with size 14 feet. His pride when he tried on the clumsy shoes was enormous. His relief was greater when a letter from Dian produced custom boots made in Pennsylvania.

Not surprisingly, the camp itself was a haven for wildlife. Dian got an orphaned dog, Cindy, from friends "down below." Cindy was indulged like a house pet by everyone in camp.

IT WAS IMPOSSIBLE TO FEEL LONELY."

▲ *Dian shares breakfast with one of the white-necked ravens that arrived each morning for a handout.*

▲ *Each day when Dian went tracking, Cindy would proudly lead her into the forest for a half mile or so. Then a woodsman would take Cindy back to safely "stand guard" over the camp.*

Dian confiscated a monkey from a
poacher and brought it home. Kima became
a long-term companion and troublemaker,
forever tearing things apart.

Dian kept chickens and geese. Some forest
animals became such regular visitors that
she named them.

No animal was ever turned away by the
woman who never had pets as a child.

Peanuts experimented with Dian's tools,
even taking her binoculars and looking through them
backwards to get microscopic views of insects in the grass.
One gorilla sat entranced flipping through the pages of
NATIONAL GEOGRAPHIC magazine, inspecting photographs of
his friends for hours. She gave the females of Group 4 a
mirror. They marvelled at themselves while the males hooted
with displeasure.

She wrote about all of the gorillas like family, but she was
closest to Digit.

*►After its morning meal, Group 4
spreads out to rest and digest. Much
of the vegetation they eat, such as wild
celery and bamboo stalks, is very rough
and fibrous. Because mountain gorillas
eat up to 70 pounds of fiber a day,
they need to spend lots of time digesting.*

On warm sunny days when group contentment is at its highest....[it] is an extraordinary feeling to be able to sit in the middle of a resting group of gorillas...."

▼Dian shared Digit's curiosity about almost everything.

Digit and Dian were special friends. They sat back to back in the grass; she rested her head in his lap, he stroked her hair. They talked to each other through long eye contact. She photographed him endlessly and was as proud of Digit as a mother might be.

He was a sentry, always looking for danger that might leap out of the forest. And he took that job more seriously than any other gorilla Dian knew. She wrote, "Digit has become a 'big man' now, and you'd be proud of the way he helps Uncle Bert look after the group."

▶ *This four-year-old could have lived to 40 if she hadn't wandered into a poacher's trap set to catch antelope. After getting free of the trap, her mangled leg became so badly infected that she died from gangrene.*

Karisoke was a success, a center for vital research, an exciting place to live and work. But the poaching of protected animals continued. And poaching caused conflict between Dian and the students. Most objected to doing anti-poaching work: rooting traps out of the brush, chasing cattle out of the gorilla park, hunting down and questioning suspects.

Students had to help stop poaching if they wanted to stay. Dian was absolute about that.

On the other hand, she could not treat the poachers as harshly as she would have liked to treat them. She knew that the $20 or so that a trader paid for gorilla heads or hands was a fortune to a poacher and his family. But to Dian, poachers were murderers and deserved prison for life.

Gradually, unintentionally, Dian slipped into war with everybody who threatened the gorillas.

After Cindy was kidnapped twice, Dian took a herd of cattle hostage. Kima was kidnapped and the chickens were poisoned—all to threaten her. Dian retaliated by shooting at cattle grazing illegally in the park and by raiding poachers' camps and villages. She stole poachers' weapons and clothing, even burned their camps. Several suspects were tied up and threatened until they confessed.

If students complained about her tactics, she branded them as weak.

▲ *Dian and the staff destroyed thousands of traps and snares, but could never stop poachers from setting new traps.*

The poachers' attacks from without and student criticism from within wore on her. She isolated herself from people, staying alone in her cabin.

Then, on January 2, 1978, Ian Redmond, long-term student and friend, walked hesitantly up to Dian and told her the most devastating news she had ever heard. Digit had been killed. His body was riddled with spear wounds; his head and hands had been hacked off.

Poachers had surprised Group 4 a few days earlier. Uncle Bert, the leader, had rallied his family and led them off to safety. Digit stayed behind, screaming and charging at the attackers. He bought time for the group's escape, but had no chance against spears and machetes.

Desolate but not beaten, Dian counterattacked. She increased

54

anti-poaching activities. She started the Digit Fund to publicize the gorillas' plight and raise money for more anti-poaching patrols. Active conservation was now her prime objective.

The war escalated, and her enemies grew in number.

Then poachers shot Uncle Bert, the leader of Group 4, and his mate. A wounded infant died shortly after.

Digit, Uncle Bert, and the others were buried in the gorilla graveyard near Dian's cabin. Originally for gorillas who died from natural causes, it was now filling up with casualties of war. And Dian, herself, was imperiled.

There was growing opposition to her management of Karisoke. Even the U.S. State Department was concerned because of the complaints against her by the government of Rwanda.

Much of the world conservation community believed that controlled tourist access would save and protect the gorillas. Dian believed that tourism would threaten long-term gorilla safety for short-term gain.

By 1980, Dian was frustrated, angry, and physically worn out. She called herself Fossil Fossey. She had survived rabies, sprains, and broken bones but nagging hip-and-back pain disabled her now. Stuck in camp, she called her cabin The Mausoleum.

Dian temporarily gave up the directorship of Karisoke in August 1980. Reluctantly, she returned to the United States.

▶ *Dian writes Digit's name on his grave marker.*

▶ *Rwandese neighbors turn out to wish Dian good luck as she leaves Karisoke for the United States in August 1980.*

"I'VE LEARNED TO REMEMBER TO FLUSH
THE TOILET AND HOW TO TURN ON THE LIGHTS....FOR SURE, LIFE ISN'T
AS SIMPLE IN THE STATES AS IN RWANDA!"

▲Dr. Leakey's "Ape Ladies" (from left to right):
Dian Fossey, Jane Goodall, and Biruté Galdikas,
who studied orangutans in Indonesia, were very
popular public speakers.

▲Professor Fossey
prepares a lecture.
Behind her are
portraits of some of
the friends she left
behind.

At age 48, Dr. Dian Fossey became a visiting associate professor
at Cornell University, in Ithaca, New York. Cindy, her aged mutt,
moved with her. When not occupied with writing lectures, running
the Digit Fund, or learning how to live again in the U.S., she
worked on *Gorillas in the Mist*—a book about her life's work.
Surgery relieved her agonizing back-and-hip pain.

She dove into academic life and was voted Best Teacher on
Campus by her students. She had a salary for the first time in nearly
20 years, but longed to return to what she called "my real home."

In 1983, Dian returned to Africa as director of Karisoke.
She had to accept tourism, but wanted it strictly controlled. The
Rwandan tourist board was openly hostile to her. They wanted her
to stop anti-poaching patrols and approve unlimited tourism.
It was an edgy, frustrating time, but nothing new for Dian. The
government gave her two-month visas, so much of her time was
spent in town on government paperwork.

W HEN YOU REALIZE THE VALUE OF ALL LIFE,

YOU DWELL LESS ON WHAT IS PAST AND CONCENTRATE

MORE ON THE PRESERVATION OF THE FUTURE."

After *Gorillas in the Mist* was published in September of 1983, Dian did several promotional tours. By 1984, the book had been translated into six languages. A Hollywood movie deal was signed, and Sigourney Weaver was hired to play Dian.

Dian was offered speaking engagements and endorsements. Advertisers wanted her to appear in commercials.

Fame and money couldn't lure her heart away from Karisoke. She wrote: "I know that I've truly come home again. No one will ever force me out of here again."

In December 1985, her wishes for peace with the local government came true. A friend of Rwanda's leader renewed her visa for a full two years. "The Big Man handed it to me with a laugh and said the next one would be for ten years if I wanted. Wow, if he handed me a ticket to Cloud Nine I couldn't have been happier."

Dian decorated her cabin for the Christmas celebration, but postponed it until the New Year. The party never happened.

Dian's body was discovered the morning of December 27, 1985. An unknown person or persons had entered her cabin during the night and crushed her skull with a panga. She tried to defend herself, but there were no bullets in her revolver.

Dian's murder was investigated. Who killed her and why she was killed are questions still unanswered today.

Dian Fossey's African friends buried her in the gorilla graveyard, nearest to Digit.

Her spirit and strength live on, like a light shining through the mist.

▶ *Dian's final journal entry, quoted above, was written in her Karisoke cabin on or about December 25, 1985.*

A F T E R W O R D

▶ *Today, a Rwandese park worker observes and makes notes on gorilla behavior.*

In the 1970s, Rwandese were asked to describe gorillas. The majority couldn't think of a single adjective for gorillas because almost no Rwandese ever saw living gorillas. They thought of gorillas purely as a nuisance.

Volcanoes National Park was prime farming, cattle-grazing, and hunting land that Rwandese needed for survival. Protecting the gorillas was the furthest thing from the peoples' minds. And most park administrators had no conservation training; they were political appointees trying to make a living. Sometimes they paid poachers to capture or kill the animals they were supposed to protect.

That's nearly all changed today.

Thanks to educational programs run by conservation organizations and the Karisoke Research Center, Rwandese think very differently about mountain gorillas —they are a national resource. It's an honor to be a park guard today. Guards will not even allow tourists with colds near gorilla habitat for fear the gorillas will be infected.

The recently discovered mountain gorillas of Uganda's Bwindi Impenetrable Forest have a large and protected habitat.

Mountain gorillas are big business today. They are bringing tourist money to countries where foreign currency and jobs are needed and welcomed.

There are no guarantees that the mountain gorilla will survive forever as a species. But there is much less chance that they will be wiped out by human greed or indifference.

Would these changes have happened without Dian Fossey? Did she really have to abandon pure science and become a combatant?

George Schaller, the first person to live among gorillas, thought that Dian did what had to be done: "Her priority was correct: When the existence of a rare creature is threatened, a conservation effort becomes primary, science secondary. Silently, as if entombed by fog, the Virunga gorillas might have retreated into oblivion had not Dian Fossey drawn international attention to their renewed plight."

CHRONOLOGY

1932   Dian Fossey born in San Francisco on January 16

1949   Graduates high school; Studies business at Marin Junior College

1950   Enters University of California as pre-veterinary major

1954   Graduates San Jose State College with a B.A. in occupational therapy

1956   Hired as Director of Occupational Therapy,
Kosair Children's Hospital, Louisville, Kentucky

1963   Travels to Africa; Meets Dr. Louis S. B. Leakey; Encounters
mountain gorillas

1966   Begins field study at Kabara, in the Democratic Republic of the Congo
(later Zaire, now Democratic Republic of the Congo again)

1967   Congolese Civil War; Establishes Karisoke Research Center with one
employee in Volcanoes National Park, Rwanda

1969   Coco and Pucker come to Karisoke

1970   Peanuts touches Dian's hand; NATIONAL GEOGRAPHIC cover story; Dian
begins study at Cambridge University, in Cambridge, England

1974   Receives Ph.D. in zoology

1978   Digit and Uncle Bert are killed; Digit Fund created

1980   Dian resigns directorship of Karisoke; Becomes visiting
associate professor at Cornell University, in Ithaca, New York

1983   Dian returns to Karisoke as Director in June; *Gorillas in the Mist* published

1985   Dian murdered at Karisoke

1990s Karisoke closed several times by war; Dian's cabin burned; Karisoke
Research Center fully operational in 1997, with 36 full-time employees

Dian Fossey's quotes are taken from her journals and letters that appear in *Woman in the Mists*, from *Gorillas in the Mist*, and from her NATIONAL GEOGRAPHIC articles, all cited below.

▶ *A Rwandese child proudly displays his drawing of happy gorillas being photographed by tourists.*

Akeley, Carl. *In Brightest Africa*. New York: Doubleday, 1923.

Baumgartel, Walter. *Up Among the Mountain Gorillas*. New York: Hawthorne Books, 1976.

Bourne, Geoffrey H. and Cohen, Maury. *The Gentle Giants*. New York: G.P. Putnam's Sons, 1975.

Cavalieri, Paola and Singer, Peter (eds.). *Great Ape Project*. New York: St. Martin's Press, 1994.

Fossey, Dian. *Gorillas in the Mist*. Boston: Houghton Mifflin, 1983.

———. 1970. "Making Friends with Mountain Gorillas." NATIONAL GEOGRAPHIC 137 No. 1: 48–67.

———. 1971. "More Years with Mountain Gorillas." NATIONAL GEOGRAPHIC 140 No. 4: 574–85.

———. 1981. "The Imperiled Mountain Gorilla." NATIONAL GEOGRAPHIC 159 No. 4: 501–23.

Goodall, Alan. *The Wandering Gorillas*. London: William Collins Sons, 1979.

Groves, Colin P. *Gorillas*. New York: Arco Publishing, 1970.

Hayes, Harold T. P. *The Dark Romance of Dian Fossey*. New York: Simon & Schuster, 1990.

Montgomery, Sy. *Walking with the Great Apes*. Boston: Houghton Mifflin, 1991.

Mowat, Farley. *Woman in the Mists*. New York: Warner Books, 1987.

Nichols, Michael and Schaller, George B. *Gorilla: Struggle for Survival in the Virungas*. New York: Aperture Foundation, 1989.

Norton, Boyd. *The Mountain Gorilla*. Stillwater, MN: Voyageur Press, 1990.

Salopek, Paul F. "Gorillas and Humans: An Uneasy Truce." NATIONAL GEOGRAPHIC 188 No. 4: 72–83.

Schaller, George B. *The Year of the Gorilla*. Chicago: University of Chicago Press, 1964.

———. 1995. "Gentle Gorillas, Turbulent Times." NATIONAL GEOGRAPHIC 188 No. 4: 65–68.

FOR FURTHER INFORMATION:

The Dian Fossey
Gorilla Fund Interna-
tional
800 Cherokee Ave., S.E.
Atlanta, GA 30315
800-851-0203

If you have internet
access, try these sites
on the World Wide
Web. Each site has links
to other pages with
information about other
primates, conservation,
and a variety of envi-
ronmental subjects.

*Dian Fossey Gorilla
Fund International*
www.gorillafund.org *or*
gorilla.rutgers.edu/
content.html

Great Ape Project
www.envirolink.org/
orgs/gap/gaphome.html

*National Geographic
Society*
www.nationalgeographic.
com

*Wildlife Conservation
Society*
www.wcs.org

World Wildlife Fund
www.wwf.org

▶ *A gorilla likeness
now graces Rwanda's
1,000 franc note, an
unthinkable idea
before Dian Fossey
founded Karisoke.*

INDEX

The world's largest nonprofit scientific and educational organization, the National Geographic Society was founded in 1888 "for the increase and diffusion of geographic knowledge." Fulfilling this mission, the Society educates and inspires millions every day through magazines, books, television programs, videos, maps and atlases, research grants, the National Geography Bee, teacher workshops, and innovative classroom materials.

The Society is supported through membership dues and income from the sale of its educational products. Call 1-800-NGS-LINE for more information. Visit our Web site: www.nationalgeographic.com